FAST FOOD
WORKSHOP

Building a Menu of Quick Dishes

Megan Borgert-Spaniol

An imprint of Abdo Publishing
abdobooks.com

ABDOBOOKS.COM

Published by Abdo Publishing, a division of ABDO, PO Box 398166, Minneapolis, Minnesota 55439. Copyright © 2024 by Abdo Consulting Group, Inc. International copyrights reserved in all countries. No part of this book may be reproduced in any form without written permission from the publisher. Abdo & Daughters™ is a trademark and logo of Abdo Publishing.

Printed in the United States of America, North Mankato, Minnesota
052023
092023

Design: Aruna Rangarajan and Emily O'Malley, Mighty Media, Inc.
Production: Mighty Media, Inc.
Editor: Ruthie Van Oosbree
Recipes: Megan Borgert-Spaniol
Cover Photographs: Mighty Media, Inc.; Shutterstock Images
Interior Photographs: iStockphoto, pp. 5 (bottom), 9, 11 (top right, bottom right, bottom left), 12 (all), 13 (middle right, middle left, bottom left), 15 (middle left, bottom right, top), 16 (top right, bottom right, top left), 17 (middle right, bottom left), 18, 19 (all), 20 (all), 21 (all), 23 (second to bottom left, bottom left), 24, 26, 29 (bottom), 56, 57, 58 (left, right), 59, 60; Mighty Media, Inc., pp. 25 (kneading steps), 30 (burgers), 32 (all), 33 (all), 34–35, 36 (sandwich), 38 (all), 39 (all), 40–41, 42 (tacos), 44 (all), 45 (all), 46–47, 48 (pizza), 50 (all), 51 (all), 52–53; Shutterstock Images, pp. 3, 4, 5 (top), 6 (all), 7, 8, 10, 11 (top left), 13 (bottom right, top), 14, 15 (bottom left, middle right), 16 (bottom left), 17 (bottom right, top left, top right), 18 (top), 22, 23 (top right, bottom right, second to top left, top), 25 (top, middle left, middle right, bottom right), 27 (all), 28, 29 (top), 30 (background), 36 (background), 42 (background), 48 (background), 54 (all), 55 (all), 58 (top), 61 (all)
Design Elements: Shutterstock Images

The following manufacturers/names appearing in this book are trademarks: Belmint™, Oster®, and Pyrex®

Library of Congress Control Number: 2022948837

PUBLISHER'S CATALOGING-IN-PUBLICATION DATA

Names: Borgert-Spaniol, Megan, author.
Title: Fast food workshop: building a menu of quick dishes / by Megan Borgert-Spaniol
Other title: building a menu of quick dishes
Description: Minneapolis, Minnesota : Abdo Publishing, 2024 | Series: Kitchen to career | Includes online resources and index.
Identifiers: ISBN 9781098291402 (lib. bdg.) | ISBN 9781098277864 (ebook)
Subjects: LCSH: Food--Juvenile literature. | Cooking--Juvenile literature. | Fast foods--Juvenile literature. | Convenience foods--Juvenile literature. | Quick and easy cooking--Juvenile literature. | Microwave cooking--Juvenile literature. | Occupations--Juvenile literature.
Classification: DDC 641.55--dc23

CONTENTS

Making a Career in the Kitchen 5

The Basics 7

Getting Started 11

◆ **Signature Cheeseburger** 31

◆ **Fried Chicken Sandwich** 37

◆ **Pulled Pork Tacos** 43

◆ **Pepperoni Pizza** 49

Presentation & Beyond 54

Careers in the Kitchen 57

Glossary 62

Online Resources 63

Index 64

MAKING A CAREER IN THE KITCHEN

Are you fascinated by the way breaded chicken fries up crisp and golden in hot oil? Do you love experimenting with seasoning blends for burgers or pulled pork? Can you see yourself creating quick-service menus for diners on the go? If your answer to these questions is yes, you might be suited to a career in fast food.

Becoming a fast-food professional takes training and hard work. It takes dedication to service, quality, and safety. But if you have a passion for creating fast food, you may find that the dedication comes naturally and the hard work is worthwhile.

In this book, you'll learn about the history of fast food and how it has changed over time. You'll become familiar with basic ingredients, tools, and techniques used to create quick and tasty meals. You'll practice using these ingredients, tools, and techniques in a few basic recipes. Then, you'll try your hand at following your own tastes and inspirations to modify recipes. Finally, you'll learn how you might turn your passion for cooking into a career.

Ruins in the ancient Italian city of Pompeii show historians how street vendors made and sold their food.

In 1961, White Castle became the first fast-food chain to sell 1 billion burgers.

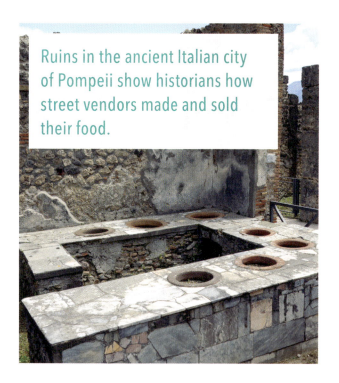
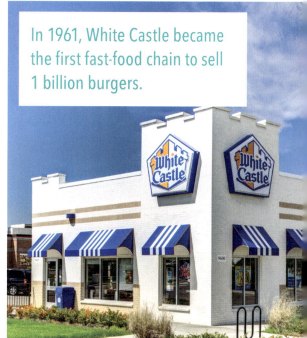

Chipotle works to provide food made using fresh ingredients without artificial flavors, colors, or preservatives.

YOU + CHIPOTLE
A BURRITOFUL COMBINATION

THE BASICS

INTRODUCTION TO FAST FOOD

The term *fast food* refers to businesses that prepare and serve food quickly and at relatively low cost. The concept of fast food dates back to street vendors in ancient Rome and during the Middle Ages. It continued with fish-and-chip shops in 1800s England. But the rise of modern fast food took place in the United States in the 1900s. To this day, fast food continues to be an iconic part of American culture.

The first modern American fast-food chain opened in 1921 in Wichita, Kansas. It was called White Castle, and it sold square hamburgers for five cents each. To speed up the cooking process and keep costs low, White Castle used the assembly-line method to make its burgers.

In 1948, California's In-N-Out Burger introduced the modern drive-through. Customers placed their orders from their cars using an intercom. Then orders were delivered through their car windows. This drive-through concept caught on and became a major part of the fast-food experience.

The 1950s saw the launch of some of the biggest names in fast food, including McDonald's. Like White Castle, McDonald's used assembly-line tactics. Each member of the kitchen staff performed a specific task, and all burgers were built with ketchup, mustard, onions, and two pickles.

As more businesses joined the fast-food scene, competition grew. Restaurants had to come up with new ways to stand out. One popular tactic was the value menu. In 1989, Wendy's was the first chain to introduce the idea, with a menu of burgers, fries, and drinks that sold for 99 cents each. Taco Bell, Burger King, and McDonald's later followed suit, offering similar value menus to customers.

Most foods at McDonald's are precooked so customers don't have to wait as long for their orders.

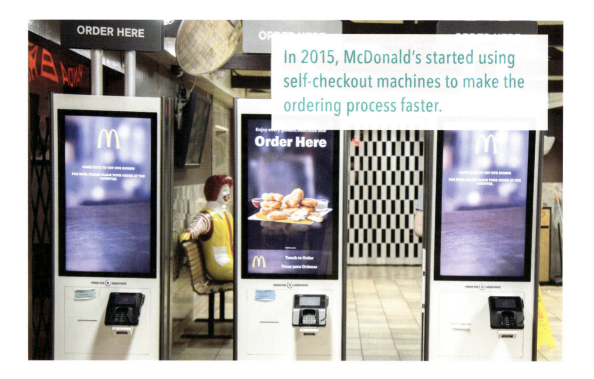

In 2015, McDonald's started using self-checkout machines to make the ordering process faster.

Low costs and speedy service made fast food a convenient option for many consumers. But it was far from the healthiest option. The industry's nutritional shortcomings became a hot topic in the 2000s. Books and documentaries helped to raise awareness of the negative health effects of fast food.

Fast-food chains responded to this awareness with new menu items that were lower in fat, sugar, and salt. McDonald's, for example, added fruit and vegetable sides to its menu. Health-conscious consumers also enjoyed new takeout options in the growing "fast-casual" dining industry. Fast-casual restaurants like Chipotle and Panera Bread offered quick service like traditional fast-food businesses, but they used fresher, less-processed ingredients.

Today, both fast-casual and traditional fast-food restaurants continue to adapt to current cultural trends. In the 2020s, these trends include plant-based diets, reducing plastic waste, and placing orders using mobile apps. No matter what the future brings, there is bound to be something for everyone in the fast-food market.

If you could build your own fast-food menu, what would you include? How would you prepare it for customers on the go? In the following pages, you'll learn about common ingredients, tools, and techniques in preparing tasty foods for quick service. Soon, you'll be a fast-food pro!

In 2021, Burger King UK shared its "Burger King for Good" plan. The plan involves improved animal welfare policies, reduced plastic waste, community support, and healthier food options.

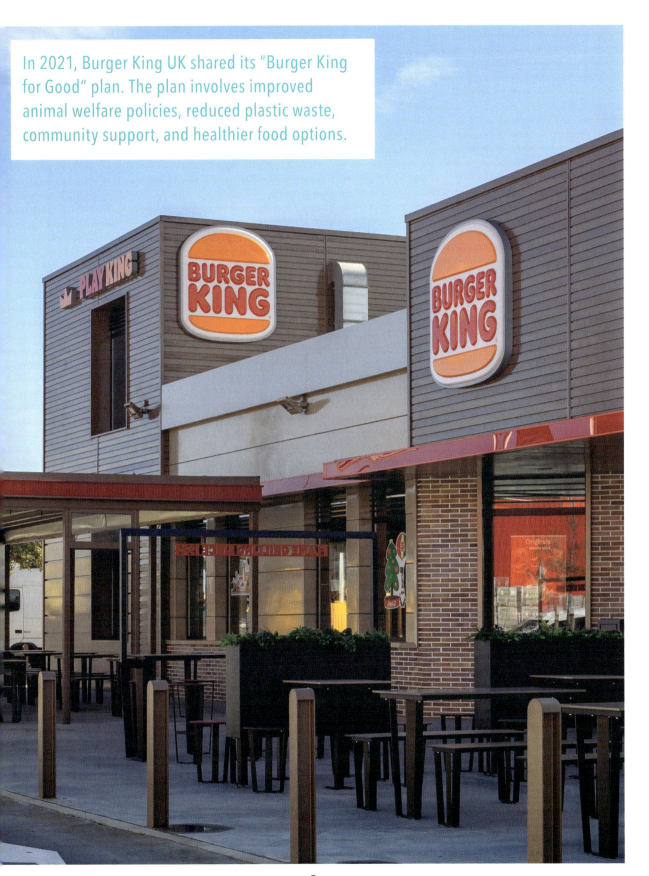

GETTING STARTED

INGREDIENTS

Get familiar with some of the ingredients you'll see in this book's recipes.

ACIDS

Buttermilk and lime juice are both acids. They are often used in marinades because they help break down proteins, which makes meats more tender. Lime wedges are also commonly served with dishes to complement rich, salty flavors.

BREADS & GRAINS

Hamburger buns come in several varieties. The recipes in this book call for brioche buns, which are enriched with butter and eggs. English muffins are bun alternatives commonly used for breakfast sandwiches. Flour tortillas are big and strong enough to wrap tightly around fillings for burritos or wraps, while the smaller, less sturdy corn tortillas are the traditional choice for tacos. Rice lays the foundation for burrito bowls.

CHEESE

Cheese comes in hundreds of varieties that range from soft and creamy to firm and salty. American cheese is a creamy processed cheese that melts easily, making it a favorite burger topper. Mozzarella is the most common pizza cheese due to its creamy texture and mild flavor.

CILANTRO

Cilantro is an herb made of the leaves and stems of the coriander plant. Its fresh, citrusy flavor pairs well with the warm spices used in many taco fillings. However, cilantro is a divisive ingredient. People with certain genes perceive a soapy taste when they eat the herb!

CONDIMENTS & SAUCES

Sauces and condiments are fast-food staples used during and after cooking. Worcestershire sauce seasons ground beef with complex sweet-and-salty flavors. Hot sauce in a chicken marinade imparts a subtle heat to the finished product. Mayonnaise provides a mild, creamy base for many fast-food signature sauces.

CORNSTARCH

Cornstarch is a fine powder made from corn. It is used as a thickening agent for sauces and soups. Cornstarch also helps make breading for foods such as chicken extra crispy when fried.

FLOUR

The recipes in this book call for all-purpose flour. This is a blend of wheat flours that can be used to make a variety of baked goods, including pizza crust. It is also used to coat chicken before frying it, resulting in a golden, crispy breading.

KOSHER SALT & BLACK PEPPER

Salt is a mineral that brings its own flavor while also enhancing other flavors. The recipes in this book call for kosher salt, which is made up of coarser grains than table salt. Black pepper comes from berries called peppercorns that are dried and ground. It adds depth and spice to all kinds of dishes.

MEAT

A "cut" of meat refers to the part of an animal the meat comes from. Different cuts are suited to different dishes. Hamburgers are typically made of ground beef chuck, which comes from the shoulder of a cow. Ground chuck marketed as "80/20," meaning it is 80 percent lean meat and 20 percent fat, is ideal for making juicy burger patties. Fried chicken sandwiches often use

chicken thighs, which have more fat and therefore a richer flavor than chicken breasts. Grilled chicken wraps use cutlets, which are made with chicken breast. Pulled pork is typically made with pork shoulder.

OIL

Oils are liquid fats used in cooking and baking. They allow foods to cook in hot pans without burning. Olive oil has a complex flavor that adds richness to foods. Vegetable oil has a neutral flavor and can withstand higher heat than olive oil, making it a great oil for frying.

PIZZA SAUCE

Pizza sauce is a thick sauce made with tomato paste and seasonings such as garlic, oregano, and basil. You can buy canned or jarred sauce at the store. But keep in mind that pizza sauce is different from tomato and pasta sauces! Pizza sauce is thicker and is typically uncooked so that its flavors can develop while baking.

PRODUCE

Burgers, sandwiches, and wraps need more than meat and bread. Cooks use a variety of produce to add flavor and texture to these menu items. Iceberg lettuce, red onion, and pickles all add crunch but impart very different flavors. Avocado brings creamy texture and a mild buttery flavor.

SPICES

Spices can add a variety of flavors to different dishes. Many are dehydrated, ground versions of the ingredients they are named after, such as onion powder and garlic powder. Chili powder and paprika bring heat. Whole and ground cumin seeds add a warm, earthy flavor. Cinnamon is also warm and earthy, but with a hint of citrus sweetness.

YEAST

Yeast is a leavening agent that makes bread dough rise. The pizza dough recipe in this book calls for fast-acting instant yeast. This dry yeast activates quickly due to its fine grain size. It is best used for doughs that require one quick rise.

KITCHEN TOOLS

Get familiar with some of the supplies you'll see in this book's recipes.

BAKING SHEET

A baking sheet is a pan with a shallow rim around all four sides or no rim at all.

BASTING BRUSH

A basting brush is a soft-bristled brush used to evenly coat pans or ingredients with oil. It is also used to spread glazes, marinades, and cooking juices over meat or vegetables. If you don't have a basting brush, you can use an unused paintbrush, a paper towel, or a silicone spatula.

COOLING RACK

A cooling rack allows air to circulate around hot food, helping it cool faster than it would on a solid surface.

DOUGH SCRAPER

A dough scraper is a rectangular piece of steel with a handle. Its dull blade end is used for dividing doughs. Some dough scrapers are made of plastic instead of metal. These are strong enough to cut through dough but also flexible enough to scrape dough out of bowls and off mixing equipment.

DUTCH OVEN

A Dutch oven is a heavy, durable pot used to cook food on the stove or in the oven. Most Dutch ovens are made of cast iron, allowing them to withstand high temperatures and retain heat. They can be used to fry chicken, slow-cook beef, and even bake bread!

GRILL PAN & GRIDDLE

A grill pan is a skillet with raised lines crossing its surface. These lines create the same char lines, or grill marks, achieved by cooking on an outdoor grill grate. Char lines add flavor and texture to grilled food. A griddle is similar but has a smooth, flat surface.

NONSTICK SKILLET

A nonstick skillet is a lightweight metal pan with a smooth inner surface. This surface is coated with a material that keeps food from sticking to the pan as it cooks.

PARCHMENT PAPER

Parchment paper is a heat-resistant nonstick paper that helps prevent ingredients, such as doughs, from sticking to baking sheets or other surfaces. Parchment paper is only good for one or two uses. If you want to avoid paper waste, a silicone baking mat does the job of parchment paper but is washable and reusable.

PIZZA CUTTER

A pizza cutter is a circular blade with a handle. It rolls like a wheel across a cutting board, creating a clean cut through pizza. Some cooks prefer to cut their pizzas with a mezzaluna, a long, curved blade that is rocked back and forth.

PIZZA PEEL

A pizza peel is a flat paddle used to transfer a pizza in and out of the oven. Generally, the pizza is assembled on the peel and then slid onto a surface in the oven. When the pizza is fully cooked, the peel slides underneath the pie to lift it out of the oven. If you don't have a peel, assemble your pizza on parchment paper, then transfer it to and from the oven using a rimless baking sheet.

PLASTIC WRAP

Plastic wrap, or cling wrap, is a thin plastic film used to cover ingredients. The wrap creates an airtight seal that prevents the ingredients from drying out in the refrigerator. It is also used to cover doughs, sometimes loosely, while they rise or rest. To avoid plastic waste, some cooks use reusable plastic bags, beeswax wrap, or cotton towels instead.

THERMOMETERS

A meat thermometer measures the internal temperature of meat and fish. For an accurate reading, insert the thermometer into the thickest part of the meat. While meat thermometers read up to about 200°F, candy thermometers and deep-fry thermometers read up to about 400°F. Both candy and deep-fry thermometers can be used to measure oil temperature.

SLOW COOKER

A slow cooker is a countertop electrical appliance used to cook food slowly over low, moist heat. It is often used to tenderize tough cuts of meat. Slow cookers are also commonly used to make soups and stews.

TONGS

Tongs are a kitchen tool made of two long metal arms joined at one end. Tongs are held in one hand and used to flip, transfer, or otherwise handle meat and other hot foods.

WHISK

A whisk is used to blend ingredients quickly and thoroughly. This includes dry ingredients, such as for dry rubs and breading mixtures, and wet ingredients, such as for sauces and marinades.

TERMS & TECHNIQUES

Get familiar with some of the terms and techniques you'll see in this book's recipes.

CHOPPING VERSUS DICING

Chopping is a cutting technique that results in rough, uneven chunks of an ingredient (*top*). Dicing is a more precise cutting technique that results in slightly smaller pieces of uniform size (*bottom*).

DRY RUB

A dry rub is a blend of spices and other seasoning ingredients that is rubbed onto the surface of meat or other foods before cooking. Dry rubs add flavor to the meat without adding moisture.

FLOURING THE WORK SURFACE

Most recipes call for doughs to be rolled out on a floured surface. Start with a light, even sprinkle of flour over a clean, dry surface. If the dough starts to stick, sprinkle a little more flour onto the surface. Don't add too much! Otherwise, it will be harder to shape the dough.

MAKING A WELL

A common technique when mixing doughs is to form a well, or crater, in the dry ingredients before pouring the wet ingredients into the well. The dry ingredients are then gently incorporated into the well of wet ingredients until a dough forms.

GRILLING

Grilling is cooking food at a high temperature while exposing it directly to the heat source. Grates create distinctive char lines, or grill marks, on the surface of the food. Grilling is often done outdoors with a charcoal, gas, or electric grill. But cooks can also use indoor grill appliances and stovetop grill pans to achieve a similar effect.

MARINATING

Marinating is soaking meat, fish, or vegetables in a liquid solution called a marinade before cooking. Marinades help flavor the food. They also usually contain acids, such as buttermilk or citrus juice, that help tenderize the food.

RESTING DOUGH

Letting bread dough rest allows the gluten, an elastic protein that forms during kneading, to relax. This makes the dough easier to roll out or otherwise shape.

RESTING MEAT

Large cuts of meat continue cooking for a few minutes after they are removed from their heat source. So, letting the meat rest allows it to reach its peak temperature. Additionally, cutting into freshly cooked meat will cause its juices to spill out. But when given time to rest, the meat will fully absorb this moisture, making it tender and juicy.

PAN DRIPPINGS

Pan drippings are the juices that collect at the bottom of a pan while cooking meat. Pan drippings can be used to make sauces, moisten cooked meat, flavor roasted vegetables, and more.

PREHEATING THE OVEN

Pizza dough and other baked goods rely on an initial blast of heat to kick-start their rise. That's why it's important to preheat your oven, or let it fully heat to the specified temperature, before you start baking.

SIMMERING VERSUS BOILING

If a recipe says to heat a liquid to a simmer, look for small bubbles that rise to the liquid's surface, causing gentle movement. If a recipe calls for boiling the liquid, look for many large bubbles rising at once, constantly disrupting the liquid's surface.

VENTING

Filled doughs such as calzones require vents, or slits, cut into the dough. This allows steam to escape as the dough bakes.

SEASONING WITH SALT & PEPPER

Without salt and pepper, most dishes would taste bland. But too much salt and pepper will overpower the other flavors in the dish. Finding the right balance takes some trial and error. If a recipe says simply to season your ingredients, start with a generous pinch of salt and a smaller pinch of pepper. Try to taste your ingredients throughout the cooking process to ensure they are properly seasoned.

KITCHEN PREP TIPS

> Have all your supplies out and ready before you begin. Gather all your ingredients on a tray or rimmed baking sheet. Then it's easy to slide everything out of the way if you need to make space.
> Wear an apron to protect your clothing. It will also serve as a hand towel.

INGREDIENT PREP TIPS & TRICKS

Fast-food cooks spend much of their time preparing ingredients for later. That way, when orders come in, meals can be assembled quickly. Here are a few food prep tips and tricks for the recipes in this book.

Make sure the blade of your knife is sharp. A dull blade is more dangerous than a sharp one because it requires more force to cut through ingredients.

When possible, portion out ingredients ahead of time based on the amounts needed for one meal. For example, you might slice grilled chicken and divide it into separate containers.  When you need to make a chicken wrap, you can pull one container out of the refrigerator.

Fresh lettuce should be washed before eating. Swish it around in a large bowl of cold water, then let it float for about 30 seconds before  taking it out. This lets any dirt or sand on the lettuce sink down to the bottom of the bowl. This same method can be used to wash leafy herbs such as cilantro.

To avoid soggy lettuce in burgers, sandwiches, and wraps, thoroughly dry lettuce after washing it.  A salad spinner is a great tool for this. If you don't have a spinner, lay the lettuce on a towel in a single layer and let it air-dry. This same method can be used to dry leafy herbs.

Cut an avocado in half along its length by running your knife around the  pit in the middle of the fruit. Pull the two halves apart. Then tap the blade of the knife into the pit and pull the pit out of the avocado.

KNEADING BASICS

Making pizza crust or any other bread from scratch usually requires some kneading. Kneading techniques vary across recipes and cooks, but a basic push-and-fold movement is a good starting point for most doughs, including the pizza dough in this book.

KITCHEN PREP TIPS

- Push the heel of your hand into the dough ball so it moves away from you along the surface.

- Fold the far edge of the dough over itself and back toward you. Rotate the dough ball slightly before the next heel push.

- Continue kneading until the dough is smooth and bounces back when you poke it. This can take 10 to 15 minutes.

- Make sure your prep surface is clean and dry. Wash your hands with soap and water both before and after you handle ingredients.

- Don't eat uncooked eggs or meat. Thoroughly wash your hands and all surfaces after handling raw meat.

- Place any leftover ingredients into containers with lids. Use tape and markers to label the container with the date and the ingredient. Then keep it somewhere you will easily see it so you don't forget about it.

CREATING IN THE KITCHEN

Recipes are great for learning how to cook. But as you get comfortable following recipes, you might start imagining ways to improve them.

Maybe you want to add caramelized onions to your burger. Or maybe you decide to use orange juice instead of lime juice in your pulled pork recipe.

This book includes four formal fast-food recipes meant to help you practice working with different ingredients and techniques. Following each formal recipe is an informal companion. These companion recipes are less structured and provide fewer details. This leaves room for you, the cook, to follow your own tastes and preferences. If an informal recipe doesn't suit your taste, check out the accompanying "Experiment!" sidebar for additional ideas. With some thought and creativity, you can make any recipe your own way.

CONVERSION CHART

Standard	Metric
¼ teaspoon	1.25 mL
½ teaspoon	2.5 mL
1 teaspoon	5 mL
1 tablespoon	15 mL
¼ cup	60 mL
⅓ cup	80 mL
½ cup	125 mL
⅔ cup	160 mL
¾ cup	175 mL
1 cup	240 mL
165°F	74°C
350°F	180°C
375°F	190°C
400°F	200°C
450°F	230°C

RULES TO REMEMBER

As you start putting your own twist on recipes, keep these guiding principles in mind.

Master the basics first. Start out following recipes exactly as they are written. You'll better understand how ingredients combine and behave, and this knowledge will inform your decisions as you go off-book.

Every cook has their own methods. You might see another cook season pork with a different blend of spices. Or, another cook may let their pizza dough rise longer than you do. This doesn't mean you have to change your ingredients or techniques. If you can, ask cooks why their methods work for them. Test the methods yourself and decide what works best for you!

Experiments don't always go to plan. Don't be crushed if you overcooked your chicken or underseasoned your beef. If the results are still edible, don't let them go to waste! Instead, think of how you can make them tastier. If your chicken is dry, top it with extra sauce or add it to a soup. If your burger tastes bland, top it with bacon, salty cheese, jalapeños, or any other ingredient that brings strong flavor.

Cooking is often called an art, not a science. A recipe won't be ruined by an extra hit of cumin or a missed teaspoon of chili powder. Cooks are always tweaking and testing their recipes. Enjoy the process and take pride in the results.

MAKE THIS!

SIGNATURE CHEESEBURGER

The cheeseburger is one of the most iconic American fast foods. Different fast-food establishments put their own spins on the burger by using different seasoning blends, signature sauces, and add-ons.

INGREDIENTS

- 1 pound (½ kg) ground beef chuck (80 percent lean)
- ½ teaspoon kosher salt, plus more for seasoning
- ¼ teaspoon ground pepper, plus more for seasoning
- 1 tablespoon Worcestershire sauce
- olive oil for brushing
- American cheese slices
- ¼ cup mayonnaise
- 2 tablespoons ketchup
- ½ tablespoon yellow mustard
- 6 brioche hamburger buns
- iceberg lettuce
- sliced red onion
- sliced pickles

SUPPLIES

- mixing bowls
- measuring cup and spoons
- gloves (optional)
- parchment paper
- jar that is slightly wider than diameter of buns
- grill pan or griddle
- stove
- basting brush
- spatula
- plate
- paper towel (optional)
- whisk
- spoon or spreading knife
- knife and cutting board

1

In a mixing bowl, combine the beef, ½ teaspoon salt, ¼ teaspoon pepper, and Worcestershire sauce. Work the seasoning ingredients into the beef with your hands, wearing gloves if desired.

2

Divide and shape the beef into six balls of equal size. Place them onto a sheet of parchment.

3

Place a second sheet of parchment over the beef balls. Use the bottom of the jar to flatten the balls into patties that are the same diameter as the jar. Then peel off the top sheet of parchment.

4 Heat the grill pan to high heat. Season both sides of each patty with salt and pepper. Then brush both sides with olive oil.

5

Place the patties on the heated pan so they are not touching each other (you will likely be able to cook two or three patties at a time). Let the patties grill undisturbed for about three minutes or until the edges are browned.

6

Flip the patties and place a slice of cheese over each. Let the patties cook for another three minutes before transferring them to a plate. If you need to grill more patties, first use a paper towel to remove extra fat from the pan. Be careful, it's hot!

7 In a small bowl, whisk together the mayonnaise, ketchup, and mustard. Season the sauce with salt and pepper.

8

Spread about 1 tablespoon of sauce over the top halves of the buns. On the bottom halves, stack two layers of lettuce and a few slices of red onion.

9 Place the patties over the onions on each bun. Then top the burgers with sliced pickles and the top halves of the buns.

MAKE IT YOUR WAY

BREAKFAST BURGER

Many fast-food businesses have successfully introduced breakfast menus to bring in more customers outside of the lunch and dinner hours. The most popular fast-food breakfast offerings are handheld items, like this breakfast burger.

Shape your seasoned beef into smaller portions than you would to make a cheeseburger. Flatten them to be slightly wider than the diameter of an English muffin.

EXPERIMENT!

Swap out the beef for a sausage patty or a couple strips of bacon. Try cooking the eggs in the microwave instead of on a pan. Instead of an English muffin, bookend your sandwich with pancakes or waffles!

After grilling the burgers, fry eggs in the leftover pan grease.

Spread a blend of mayonnaise and hot sauce onto the halves of a toasted English muffin. Stack a burger, cheese, fried egg, and some avocado slices between the two halves.

MAKE THIS!

FRIED CHICKEN SANDWICH

Chicken is another fast-food staple, especially the irresistibly crunchy fried chicken sandwich. In this recipe, spicy mayo and sour pickles balance out the chicken.

INGREDIENTS

- 4 boneless chicken thighs
- 2 teaspoons kosher salt, plus more for seasoning
- black pepper for seasoning
- 1 cup buttermilk
- 1 egg
- 1 tablespoon hot sauce
- 1 cup all-purpose flour
- ½ cup cornstarch
- 1 tablespoon garlic powder
- ½ tablespoon paprika
- vegetable oil
- ½ cup mayonnaise
- 2 tablespoons pickle juice
- 4 brioche hamburger buns
- sliced pickles
- iceberg lettuce

SUPPLIES

- knife and cutting board
- mixing bowls
- whisk
- measuring cups and spoons
- tongs
- plastic wrap
- refrigerator
- plate
- Dutch oven
- stove
- meat and deep-fry thermometers
- cooling rack
- paper towels
- spoon or spreading knife

1 Use a knife to remove any bits of fat or cartilage from the chicken thighs. Season both sides of the chicken thighs with salt and pepper.

2

In a mixing bowl, whisk together the buttermilk, egg, and ½ tablespoon hot sauce.

3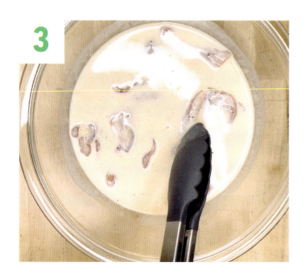

Place the seasoned thighs in the marinade. Cover the bowl with plastic wrap and refrigerate for an hour.

4 In another mixing bowl, whisk together the flour, cornstarch, garlic powder, paprika, and 2 teaspoons of salt.

5

After the chicken is done marinating, transfer the thighs one at a time into the flour mixture and coat each completely. Set the coated thighs on a plate.

6 Fill the Dutch oven with about 1 inch (2.5 cm) of oil and heat it over medium-high heat until the thermometer reads 350°F.

7

Carefully place two thighs into the hot oil. Cook the thighs for 12 to 15 minutes, turning them with tongs every few minutes, until they are golden brown and have an internal temperature of 165°F.

8

Place the cooling rack over a few layers of paper towels, which will absorb dripping grease. Then place the cooked thighs on the cooling rack.

9 Repeat steps 7 and 8 to cook the remaining thighs.

10 In a small bowl, whisk together the mayonnaise, ½ tablespoon hot sauce, and pickle juice. Season with salt and pepper.

11 Spread about 1 tablespoon of the sauce over both the top and bottom halves of the buns.

12

Place pickle slices and the fried chicken onto the bottom halves of the buns. Top the chicken with two layers of lettuce and the top halves of the buns.

MAKE IT YOUR WAY

GRILLED CHICKEN WRAP

A grilled chicken wrap is a more nutritious alternative to the fried chicken sandwich. Play around with different fillings to achieve the perfect balance of flavors and textures!

Season chicken breast cutlets with salt and pepper. Brush a hot grill pan with vegetable oil and grill the cutlets for about five minutes on each side, or until they are cooked through.

EXPERIMENT!

Add crispy bacon to your wrap for extra saltiness or avocado for creaminess. Swap out the ranch for a different type of dressing. Or go vegetarian by leaving out the meat and packing the wrap with crunchy vegetables!

Spread mayonnaise over a flour tortilla and line the tortilla with lettuce. Slice the cooked chicken into strips and place them on top of the lettuce. Top the chicken with shredded cheese, ranch dressing, and sliced tomato.

Roll the tortilla into a wrap, slice down the middle, and serve!

MAKE THIS!

PULLED PORK TACOS

Tacos fit comfortably in one hand, making them an ideal on-the-go meal. Fill them with slow-cooked pork and top with fresh onion and cilantro.

INGREDIENTS

- 1 tablespoon brown sugar
- 1½ teaspoons kosher salt
- ½ teaspoon cinnamon
- 1 teaspoon chili powder
- 1 teaspoon garlic powder
- 1 teaspoon onion powder
- 1½ teaspoons cumin
- ¼ teaspoon black pepper
- 2 pounds (1 kg) pork shoulder
- 1 tablespoon lime juice
- ½ white onion
- 1 bunch cilantro
- 1 lime
- corn tortillas

SUPPLIES

- small bowls
- whisk
- measuring spoons
- knife and cutting board
- slow cooker
- forks
- nonstick skillet
- stove
- clean kitchen towel
- tongs

1

In a small bowl, whisk together the brown sugar, salt, cinnamon, chili powder, garlic powder, onion powder, cumin, and black pepper. This is a dry rub.

2

Cut the pork into 4-inch (10 cm) chunks and place them in the slow cooker.

3

Sprinkle the lime juice and dry rub over the meat. Use your hands to toss the meat, making sure all pieces are covered with the rub.

4 Place the cover on the slow cooker and cook the meat on low for eight to ten hours.

5

When the meat is cooked and tender, take it out of the slow cooker. Let it rest for 15 minutes. Then use two forks to pull it apart into smaller pieces. Keep the pulled pork warm in the slow cooker with a little bit of the pan drippings to keep it moist.

6

Dice the onion and chop the cilantro. Cut the lime into quarter wedges, then cut each wedge in half. Place the onion, cilantro, and limes into separate bowls for easy access.

7

Heat the corn tortillas on a dry nonstick skillet over medium-high heat. Wrap the towel around the heated tortillas to keep them warm.

8 It's time to assemble! Use tongs to place the pulled pork across the center of the tortilla. Top the meat with onion and cilantro. Serve the tacos with the prepared lime wedges for squeezing.

[MAKE IT YOUR WAY]

BURRITO BOWL

Instead of tortillas, serve your pulled pork in bowls with rice, beans, cheese, and more!

Heat two parts water and one part rice in a pot until it comes to a boil. Add a pinch of salt and reduce the heat so the water comes to a simmer. Cover and cook the rice until all the water is absorbed.

EXPERIMENT!

Play with different spice combinations in your pulled pork recipe. Try making a homemade salsa or guacamole to top your bowl. For more of a salad, replace the rice with shredded lettuce.

Scoop rice into a serving bowl. Drain and rinse a can of beans. Add a scoop of the beans to the bowl along with some pulled pork.

Finish your bowl with whatever toppings you'd like, from diced onion and tomato to cheese and sour cream.

[MAKE THIS!]

PEPPERONI PIZZA

Some fast-food restaurants sell pizzas whole or by the slice. A pizza can be shaped, topped, and baked in a matter of minutes.

INGREDIENTS

- 4 cups all-purpose flour, plus more for dusting surface
- 1 tablespoon sugar
- 2 teaspoons kosher salt
- 2 teaspoons fast-acting instant yeast
- 1½ cups warm water
- 2 tablespoons olive oil
- 2 cups pizza sauce
- 4 cups shredded mozzarella or cheese blend
- about 30 pepperoni slices

SUPPLIES

- large mixing bowl
- whisk
- measuring cups and spoons
- wooden spoon
- clean surface
- plastic wrap
- dough scraper (optional)
- oven
- parchment paper
- rolling pin (optional)
- pizza peel or rimless baking sheet
- spoon or spreading knife
- pizza cutter

1 In the mixing bowl, whisk together the flour, sugar, salt, and yeast. Make a well in the center of the mixture.

2

Pour the warm water and olive oil into the well. Use a wooden spoon to push the flour mixture into the well to moisten the flour.

3

Continue mixing everything together until a ragged dough forms.

4

Transfer the dough to a floured surface and knead it for about five minutes or until the dough is smooth. Then cover the dough with plastic wrap and let it rise for 15 minutes.

5

Divide the dough in half. Roll each half into a smooth ball. Let the dough balls rest for about 10 minutes. Meanwhile, preheat the oven to 450°F.

6

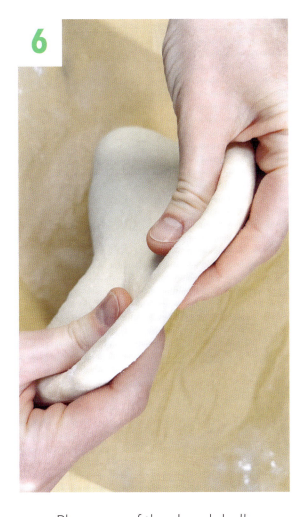

Place one of the dough balls onto a sheet of parchment paper. Use your hands to flatten the ball into an oval. Then pick up the dough by an edge and gently grab along the edges to stretch out the dough. Continue until it is a circle or oval about 10 inches (25 cm) across. If you'd like, use a rolling pin to flatten the dough.

7 Transfer the parchment and dough to a pizza peel or rimless baking sheet.

8

Spread 1 cup pizza sauce over the dough, leaving a ½-inch (1.3 cm) border uncovered. Top the sauce with 2 cups shredded cheese and about 15 slices of pepperoni.

9 Slide the parchment and pizza from the peel or sheet onto the oven rack. Bake the pizza for 15 to 20 minutes or until the crust and cheese are golden brown. Let the pizza cool before cutting it into eight slices.

10 Repeat steps 6 through 9 to make the second pizza.

MAKE IT YOUR WAY

CHEESY CALZONE

A calzone is pizza that's folded into a handheld pocket. It offers the same classic combination of ingredients in an alternative form.

Portion your pizza dough into quarters instead of halves. Roll them out into circles about ¼ inch (0.5 cm) thick. Add your chosen toppings to one half of the circle, leaving a ½-inch (1.3 cm) border along the edge.

EXPERIMENT!

Play with fun ingredient combinations, like spinach and artichokes or corn and mushrooms. Brush the unbaked calzone with butter instead of olive oil. Leave a wider border around the toppings so you have room to create a decorative seam.

Fold the pizza in half and firmly press the edges together to seal them. Brush the calzone with olive oil and sprinkle it with a pinch of salt. Cut three slits into the top of the calzone for venting.

Bake the calzone on a baking sheet lined with parchment paper for 15 to 20 minutes or until golden brown.

PRESENTATION & BEYOND

Your dish is complete, but you're not done yet! It's time to think about how you want to display or package your creation. Some fast-food establishments plate food for customers dining inside the restaurant.

Most fast-food establishments provide trays for customers dining in. This allows for easy transfer of multiple items from the service counter to the table.

Clamshell containers are a sturdier alternative to wrapping food. They often hold sauces, fries, or other sides in addition to the main meal. Clamshell containers come in many different materials, including plastic, cardboard, and Styrofoam.

Takeout bowls for salads, pastas, and similar dishes are often made of plastic or plant-based compostable materials.

SPECIAL CONSIDERATIONS

When choosing the best packaging for their food, business owners must consider several factors, including environmental impact. Aluminum, plastic, and Styrofoam are materials that take hundreds of years to decompose, if they decompose at all. As a result, products made from these materials pollute Earth's land and oceans. Because of this, many consumers choose to support businesses that package their foods in materials that decompose much faster, such as paper and cardboard. Many fast-food restaurants consider this preference when deciding how they will package their burgers, tacos, and other offerings.

Aluminum foil or plastic-coated paper are common materials for wrapping burgers, sandwiches, and tacos.

CAREERS IN THE KITCHEN

BECOMING A FAST-FOOD PROFESSIONAL

As you gain more knowledge and experience cooking quick dishes, you might decide to turn your hobby into a living. There are many ways to pursue a career in fast food!

CULINARY SCHOOL

Culinary and technical schools offer culinary arts programs that last anywhere from a few months to several years. These programs offer instruction in food science and cooking skills and prepare students for work in professional kitchens.

BUSINESS SCHOOL

Business schools offer courses in accounting, management, marketing, and other topics related to running a business. Business programs last two or more years, depending on the degree you are seeking.

ON-THE-JOB TRAINING

Most fast-food establishments hire employees with no formal culinary training. New cooks learn how to prepare the restaurant's dishes from experienced coworkers.

SELF-TEACHING

Many professional cooks and business owners learned what they know by doing their own research, watching others, making mistakes, and trying again. Entrepreneurs often follow this self-teaching path to start their own businesses.

FAST-FOOD PROS AT WORK

Fast-food professionals work in many different roles in a variety of establishments. Read about a few of them below. Think about which suit you best and why.

FAST-FOOD RESTAURANTS

Traditional fast-food restaurants emphasize their quick service and low prices. Meanwhile, less importance is placed on the quality of the food and the dining experience. Examples of these quick-service restaurants include McDonald's, KFC, Taco Bell, and In-N-Out Burger.

FAST-CASUAL RESTAURANTS

Fast-casual restaurants still offer quicker service and lower prices than full-service restaurants. However, they place more emphasis on the quality of the food and the dining experience. This makes their prices slightly higher and wait times slightly longer than those at traditional fast-food restaurants. Examples of fast-casual establishments include Shake Shack, Panera Bread, Chipotle, and Blaze Pizza.

ROLES

Fast-food establishments hire cooks to prepare the food on the menu. Large chains also hire food scientists and consultants to develop new offerings. All fast-food establishments need managers to help run daily operations. And finally, businesses need owners! Those interested in ownership can open a franchise or start their own fast-food business.

Working in a fast-food kitchen can be drastically different from home cooking. As you think about working in fast food, consider some of the tools, rules, and schedules of the industry.

TOOLS

The tools of a commercial kitchen are built to prepare large quantities of food with maximum efficiency. Commercial fryers hold vats of hot oil to cook french fries and other fried foods. Large griddles can cook more than 20 burgers at a time. Refrigerated prep tables allow quick access to sandwich fixings, pizza toppings, and other ingredients.

RULES

Fast-food professionals must uphold cleanliness and food safety standards. These standards range from wearing a uniform and keeping hair pulled back to properly storing ingredients and thoroughly cleaning equipment after use. Kitchen staff must also follow rules to protect themselves and others from common kitchen hazards, such as hot pans and wet floors.

SCHEDULES

Many fast-food establishments are open for breakfast, lunch, and dinner service. Some are open 24 hours a day. Cooks and other employees typically work shifts that are six to eight hours long. Managers and owners often work more hours.

Do What You Love!

Being a fast-food professional requires long shifts, hard physical work, and attention to rules and standards. These requirements can be difficult for home cooks to adjust to. But many professionals find the rewards of their work outweigh the difficulties. These rewards include being creative, getting exercise, and learning new skills.

Maybe your goal is to manage a quick-service kitchen. Maybe you have your sights set on opening a fast-casual operation. Or perhaps you are happy to keep cooking as a hobby but not as a career. As long as you do what you love, you'll love what you do.

GLOSSARY

appliance—a household or office device operated by gas or electric power. Common kitchen appliances include stoves, refrigerators, and dishwashers.

assembly line—a way of making products in which items move from worker to worker and each worker performs a particular task.

caramelize—to cook a food until the sugars in it brown, creating a sweet, nutty flavor.

cartilage—the soft, bendable connective tissue in the skeleton.

culinary—having to do with the kitchen or cooking.

decompose—to break down into simpler parts.

documentary—a film or television series that artistically presents facts, often about an event or a person.

edible—safe to eat.

enhance—to increase or make better.

entrepreneur—one who organizes, manages, and accepts the risks of a business or an enterprise.

establishment—a place or organization where people do business.

franchise—the right granted to someone to sell a company's goods or services in a particular place. The business operating with this right is also known as a franchise.

gluten—a protein found in many grains, such as wheat and barley.

iconic—widely recognized and well-established.

incorporate—to include or work into.

intercom—a one-way or two-way communication system allowing people to speak into a microphone and be heard on a connected device.

Middle Ages—a period in European history from about 500 CE to about 1500 CE.

plant-based—consisting of fruits, vegetables, grains, and other foods derived from plants while excluding animal products, such as meat or dairy.

shortcoming—a fault or deficiency in something.

silicone—a nontoxic substance made of silicon and oxygen atoms. It can take a rubber-like form, which is heat-resistant and used in many cooking and baking utensils.

soggy—heavy and overly moist.

technique—a method or style in which something is done.

tenderize—to make softer or easier to cut and chew.

vendor—a person or company that sells something.

ONLINE RESOURCES

To learn more about careers in fast food, please visit **abdobooklinks.com** or scan this QR code. These links are routinely monitored and updated to provide the most current information available.

INDEX

acids, 11, 19, 27, 37-38, 43-45

baking, 12-13, 15-16, 20-22, 49, 51, 53
basting brushes, 15, 31-32, 40, 52-53
beans, 46-47
boiling, 21, 46
bowls, 11, 15, 23, 31-33, 37-39, 43-47, 49-50, 55
bread, 8, 11, 13, 15, 20, 25, 31, 33-35, 37, 39, 58

careers, 5, 8, 57-59, 61
cheese, 11, 29, 31, 33-35, 41, 46-47, 49, 51-52
color, 5, 12, 33, 39, 51, 53
condiments, 7, 12, 31, 33, 35, 37, 39, 41
consumers, 7-8, 34, 54-55
cooling racks, 15, 37, 39
cornstarch, 12, 37-38

dough, 13, 15-21, 25, 29, 49-52
dough scrapers, 15, 49
drive-throughs, 7
dry rubs, 17-18, 44
Dutch ovens, 15, 37-39

eggs, 11, 25, 34-35, 37-38
England, 7
environment, 8, 55

fast-food chains, 7-8, 58
fats, 5, 8, 11-13, 15, 17, 31-33, 37-40, 49-50, 52-53, 59
flavor, 5, 8, 11-13, 16, 18-21, 27, 29, 37, 40
flour, 11-12, 18, 37-38, 49-50
fruit, 8, 11, 13, 23, 27, 40-41, 43-45, 47

grain, 11-13, 46-47
grills, 13, 16, 19, 23, 31-33, 35, 40-41

health, 8, 40
herbs, 11, 23, 43, 45

juice, 11-12, 15, 19-20, 27, 37, 39, 43-44

kneading, 20, 25, 50
knives, 18, 20-21, 23, 31, 37-38, 43-45, 49

marinating, 11-12, 15, 17, 19, 38
measuring, 17, 27, 31-33, 37-39, 43, 49, 51
meat, 5, 7, 11-13, 15, 17-20, 23, 25, 29, 31-35, 37-41, 43-46, 49, 51, 55, 58-59
menus, 5, 7-8, 13, 34, 58
Middle Ages, 7

ovens, 15-16, 20, 49-51

pans, 13, 15-16, 19-20, 22, 31-35, 40, 43, 45, 49, 51, 53, 59
pan drippings, 20, 39, 45
parchment paper, 16, 31-32, 49, 51, 53
pizza cutters, 16, 49, 51
pizza peel, 16, 49, 51
plastic wrap, 17, 37-38, 49-50, 55
plates, 31, 33, 37-38, 54

quality, 5, 8, 58

recipes
  breakfast burger, 34-35
  burrito bowl, 46-47
  cheesy calzone, 52-53
  fried chicken sandwich, 37-39
  grilled chicken wrap, 40-41
  pepperoni pizza, 49-51
  pulled pork tacos, 43-45
  signature cheeseburger, 31-33
refrigerators, 17, 23, 37-38, 59
restaurants, 7-8, 31, 49, 54-55, 57-59
resting, 17, 20, 45, 50

rolling pins, 49, 51
Rome, 7

safety, 5, 22-23, 25, 59
sauces, 12-13, 17, 20, 29, 31-33, 35, 37-39, 49, 51, 54
seasoning, 5, 8, 12-13, 18, 21, 29, 31-34, 37-40, 43-44, 49-50, 53
service, 5, 7-8, 54, 58-59, 61
simmering, 21, 46
slow cookers, 15, 17, 43-45
soup, 12, 17, 29
spatulas, 15, 31, 33
spices, 11-13, 18, 21, 29, 31-33, 37-40, 43, 46
stoves, 15, 19, 31, 33, 37-39, 43-46
sugar, 8, 43-44, 49-50

techniques, 5, 8, 18-21, 23, 25, 27, 29, 57
temperature, 5, 13, 15-17, 19-21, 32-33, 38-39, 44-46, 50-51
texture, 5, 11-13, 16, 20, 37, 40, 45
thermometers, 17, 37-39
tomato paste, 13
tongs, 17, 37-39, 43, 45
tortillas, 11, 41, 43, 45-46
towels, 15, 17, 22-23, 31, 33, 37, 39, 43, 45
training, 5, 57, 61

United States, 7, 31

vegetables, 7-8, 11-13, 15, 19-20, 23, 27, 31, 33, 37, 39-41, 43, 45-47, 52
venting, 21, 53

water, 21, 23, 25, 46, 49-50
whisks, 17, 31, 33, 37-39, 43-44, 49-50

yeast, 13, 49-50